ZARA ZAZ

Tell Depression: "NO!"

8 Saving Steps: From Depression to Joy

This book was professionally typeset on Reedsy.
Find out more at reedsy.com

Contents

Introduction

"A person suffering from depression can become an active participant in the fight against it only if he has all the necessary information."

Depression is a puzzle. In the literal and figurative sense of the word. We react to life's troubles, experience stress - severe and sudden, or outwardly insignificant, but very long, and as a result, the capabilities of our brain are depleted. After the weakened brain begins to fall into stress from any nonsense, its condition worsens further. Ultimately, a vicious circle is obtained. And how to break it, until very recently, it was absolutely incomprehensible.

Each of us in our lives has repeatedly been upset, fallen into melancholy, but not everyone knows what real depression is. When you are just upset, somewhere inside you know very well: this is temporary, this is not forever, "just unlucky", this is a non-committal failure.

That which is perceived positively by an ordinary person, that which pleases him, that which inspires confidence and hope in him, acts in the opposite way on a depressive patient. The whole world is repainted for him in black tones.

A person suffering from depression lives in another world, in another dimension, on his planet there is no faith, no hope, no love. And if the above applies to us, then until we get rid of depression, we will not believe that this life has any meaning, there will be no hope in us that we will ever be happy, we will not feel love even if we are unspeakably loved.

This book is about how to get out of depression, about ways out and means of getting out of it. Depression can and should be dealt with, because we simply have no other choice, because living with depression is toiling, but this is not life, but we must live.

Chapter 1

Depression in our lives

It is impossible to be an educated person and not know that depression is the most dangerous enemy of our civilization.

More than half of the new drugs invented in the world are psychotropic drugs, and in particular antidepressants. What does it mean? Literally the following: firstly, the problem of mental disorders is relevant and does not want to lose its relevance, and secondly, it has not yet been possible to solve it, because if a solution were found, then there would be no need for an endless invention of new psychotropic drugs.

The Nature of Depression

Depression is a mental disorder, and it has its own history, its own nature. At its core, this is a painful amplification of a normal, natural emotion for each of us - emotions of grief, sadness, suffering. Somewhere our genes let us down, and somewhere we substitute ourselves.

Nothing bad happened to me! Indeed, this is what we usually think: if a person has a misfortune, then he may have depression, and if not, then depression should not be.

In some people, depression occurs after a malfunction in the psyche due to severe mental trauma, in others it is due to a genetic predisposition, in others it is due to chronic stress.

Depression following a severe mental trauma (the death of a loved one – a child, spouse, parents) is called "reactive". And we must admit that reactive depression is a condition from which none of us is immune. If a person dies, with whom much is connected in our life, then, of course, it seriously, almost radically changes. Any change in life, regardless of its quality, is a serious stress for the psyche. But the situation worsens many times over in a situation where what happened is traumatic not only because of a malfunction in the work of the mental apparatus, but also simply because it is a real life catastrophe for a person.

The pain that a person experiences when faced with such a tragedy, the horror that he has to endure, that anxiety that pierces him when he finds out about what happened, defies any description. The intensity of these sensations and feelings is almost fatal, the tension is overwhelming. A real chaos reigns in a person's head, everything collapses in it – ideas about their future, habitual existence, social environment.

Depression that develops latently, as a consequence of perhaps less severe, but chronic stress. Such depression is more common, and, as a rule, we do not even notice how we find ourselves in its captivity.

If a real tragedy happened in our life, then everything seems to be clear – the reasons are clear. When we have chronic stress – things don't go well at work, everything is not going well at home, in addition, the doctors found some kind of disease in us - there is no one reason, our enemy seems to be blurred. Ask yourself - what's the problem? And there will be no answer. Bad, but why is unknown.

Psychological stress is not always obvious, clear, plain. We become irritable, overreact to minor problems, cannot concentrate, fuss, have difficulty sleeping, etc.

You probably know that we acquire some mental disorders for ourselves, and some arise because of heredity, that is, because of those diseased genes that came to us from our parents, the parents of our parents, etc. And genetic predisposition may play an important role in the development of our depression.

Conditions may arise in a person's life that will awaken depressive genes, and then the fight against depression will become a difficult task at all. What are these conditions? First of all, this is the same chronic stress that resulted in neurasthenia. It is he who most often turns out to be the alarm clock that awakens the depression dormant in our genes.

Chapter 2

Manifestations of depression

Each disease – both physical and mental – is characterized by a certain list of symptoms, signs indicating that it, this disease, a person has.

In addition, it is important not only to find one or another symptom of depression in yourself, but also to understand how strongly it is expressed. It directly depends on the latter what measures need to be taken to return oneself to the bosom of society with a normal, healthy mood.

Symptoms of depression are divided into "primary" and "additional". What is their difference? The primary symptoms of depression are observed in everyone who suffers from depression, although in varying degrees. Additional symptoms only complement, diversify, color the picture of the disease – in each case, some of them are present, and some are not.

So, the <u>primary symptoms of depression are</u>:

· reduced mood, feeling of despondency, depression, melancholy;

· loss of interest, ability to experience pleasure;

· decreased energy, activity, increased fatigue.

Additional symptoms of depression, although called additional, sometimes cause a person even more suffering than the main symptoms of the disease.

Additional symptoms of depression are:

· difficulty, if necessary, to concentrate, to keep attention;

· decrease in self-esteem, the emergence of a sense of self-doubt, ideas of guilt and self-abasement;

· a gloomy and pessimistic vision of the future,

· ideas or actions of self-harm and suicide;

· sleep disturbances (usually early morning awakenings);

· appetite is changed (in any direction);

· decreased libido (sexual desire);

· somatic complaints without organic causes, as well as hypochondriacal mood.

Chapter 3

8 Saving Steps:

After we have found the root of evil, after we have understood what kind of anxiety lies at the basis of our depression, it is necessary to start fighting depression itself.

Step 1: Depression inventory

We will now take a detailed inventory of our own depression. In general, when we are depressed, we are pessimistic about everything, but there are times when we seem to get drunk on our depression - and then depressive language delights simply rage out of us. Well, at such and such a moment we write down these thoughts on paper. And be sure to write it down!

However, just writing down your depressive ideology is of little use. This matter needs to be systematized immediately. We systematize in groups: the first will be what we think about the world around us, the second - about the future, the third - about ourselves. To make the task easier, we draw a table ...

What do we, being depressed, think about the world around us? There are several options, and therefore I can only report generalized thoughts of a depressed person on this matter. The world appears in depression as unfair, cruel, absurd, empty. It seems that "everything is bad" - and here we are not going well, and there we have problems, and here nothing can be achieved, and there is no need to achieve at all, because "everything is useless". We write it all down in the first column.

Now about your future. As you know, "we don't have a future." We "will not succeed", "everything will only get worse", "life will continue to be filled with the suffering and deprivation that I am experiencing now." We have "no reason to live", we have "nothing to expect", we have "nothing to count on".

Finally, a "few words about myself." We think of ourselves as: "I am nothing," "I am a loser," "I am of no use to anyone," and so on. Perhaps you blame yourself for all conceivable and unimaginable troubles. Perhaps, however, you have a slightly better opinion of yourself, but "life did not give you a chance", and therefore you "didn't work out", you "didn't achieve anything", you "didn't take place", "couldn't", "failed" .

So, we wrote down all our depressive thoughts, more specifically, what our depression makes us think. This may seem like a daunting task, but it's worth it. And in our depressed head, you can believe me, there is nothing else, everything that we think comes down to three positions.

First, let's analyze the first column that we made on the world around us, and on our life. A specific feature of these thoughts is their absolutist nature: "Nothing pleases!", "It doesn't get worse!" etc. Now we are discussing... Is it really bad that the sun has risen today? Hardly. And the fact that there are windows in the apartment is not pleasing? Better, then, without windows? No, you must admit, the windows are pleasing.

Everything is not bad. Basically! Just the fact that you are sitting, standing, lying down is not "bad", it is normal and therefore even good. If nothing monstrous is happening right now, that's also good. Regarding the phrase that "it doesn't get worse", I can assure you that it can get worse. So we obviously overdid it, and therefore we cross out this entire column.

Now "depressive thoughts about the future"... Tell me, please, which one of you knows your future? All life experience testifies: any joys and sorrows come to us unexpectedly - out of the blue. For those who are depressed, this should be especially clear. Who among them before the onset of depression thought that they would develop it? I think not many. But it has developed! Therefore, we overlooked this misfortune. Now, for some reason, we are firmly convinced that we know the future. Why?

The fact that we feel bad now does not mean that we will feel bad tomorrow. Much depends on how we proceed now. If we do something today to undermine this "depressive mindset,", won't it be easier for us tomorrow?

However, this is also unknown, but something else is known - if we do not do this today, then tomorrow we will definitely not feel better. And now this is known as precisely as the fact that the future is absolutely unknown. We can also cross out the second column.

Finally, we come to the third point, our thoughts about ourselves. The fact is that no person, unless, of course, he is already in the last stage of depressive insanity, actually thinks of himself as badly as he says about it.

In fact, we are firmly convinced that we are the best. It's just that it's not customary for us to tell others about it, and in depression we don't consider it possible to admit it to ourselves.

Imagine a person whom you do not respect, whom you consider out of his mind, eccentric and rude, insolvent and harmful to the marrow of his bones.

Now mentally put the "nasty things about yourself" from the third column of your table into the mouth of this person, the person who you would never, ever let criticize you. So, imagine that some person we hate says: "You are nothing!", "You are a loser!" Of course, a noble indignation arises in the soul, and the entire column is crossed out by us, instantly and repeatedly.

Now look at the sheet you have crossed out and come to your senses. What is written on it is sheer absurdity.

Do this procedure several times and then you will begin to notice and protest your own depressive thoughts, even without writing them out. Such rehabilitation of foci of depressive "infection" is a high-quality both therapeutic and prophylactic agent. So do not dismiss the opportunity to improve the quality of your life in such a simple way.

Step 2: Never feel sorry for yourself!

"Never feel sorry for yourself!" - this is a private, but very important rule that everyone who is going to fight their depression needs to remember. If suffering is elevated to a cult, if it commands respect, then we will never get rid of this "descent into suffering".

Suffering is impossible without self-pity. Only if we feel sorry for ourselves does suffering have a chance to torment us with all the means it has. Look behind you in a moment of despair, what is your own action that makes this moment, makes your tears? Surely this is self-pity. Get rid of self-pity, stop pitying ourselves, and our suffering will dissipate like smoke.

But as long as we feel sorry for ourselves, we are nurturing our own suffering. As long as we cherish our own suffering, we feel bad. That is why, if we really set out to improve the quality of our own lives, we need to stop feeling sorry for ourselves. So never feel sorry for yourself and never let anyone else do it. Of course, such an instruction sounds almost cruel. But in fact, it is not this tactic that is cruelty to oneself and others, but the reverse of it.

Step 3: Business - time! (or how to cheat depression)

What do we spend the day on, absorbed by our depression? It is difficult to answer this question. It is clear that this is an empty day. Either we don't want to do anything at all and we don't do it if we can. Or, what we do can only be called a "work" at a stretch, since in reality it is only an imitation of activity.

If we are depressed, we have nothing else to do: we must pull ourselves together and do something (very unpretentious) to do. Any business, any occupation will divert mental forces from depressive thoughts, and therefore their destructive effect on our state of mind will stop.

Of course, this is not a panacea, but a very important element in the complex of measures to combat depression. What you need to do is to draw up daily schedules. Staying busy is, of course, a chore, but it puts thoughts into order, and that's all we need.

So, work with the schedule. To start, sit down by the table this evening and simply write down all the things that you have done during the day. Write down absolutely everything that you can somehow name or designate. By analyzing this data, you will be able to see that during this day you repeatedly had time gaps that were not filled with anything, with any activity.

Now think about what things you can cram into tomorrow. And remember that now you should adhere to the rule: the smaller the matter, the less serious it is, the better. Make a schedule in such a way that there are no gaps in it, so that for every empty pastime you have some insignificant, but occupation. Remember - this is your plan for tomorrow, it is necessary that it is constantly at your fingertips and carried out.

The goal is not to exactly match the plan but to ensure that there are no empty slots left. At the end of what has been said, there is a caveat. You yourself know that you can do something, but at the same time think about something completely different, in particular, "drive" your depressive thoughts - from left to right and from right to left. This will not work, try to completely switch to the activity that you carry out. Try to approach any matter, even the most trifling, as thoroughly as possible.

If you are just eating, do it as if you were participating in a Japanese tea ceremony. If you're just riding public transport, keep yourself busy reading or staring. If you are talking to someone, then try to be attentive, to understand the essence of the message addressed to you.

Such simple methods of natural stimulation of the brain, along with general employment and dedication to business, can slowly, little by little, shake the brain dormant in a depressive dream. But we have it, when we are in a state of depression, it literally falls asleep, slows down, slows down. And the more active you are, the busier you are, the less likely you are to be depressed.

Step 4: Stop running!

All our thoughts can be conditionally subdivided into "forecasts", "requirements" and "explanations".

What I call "forecasts" are usually at the root of our anxieties. "Forecast" is when we mentally look into our future, and our consciousness draws pictures of various dangers and disasters for us. Of course, in such conditions it is difficult not to be alarmed.

"Requirements" are all our thoughts that begin with the words: "Must! Must! Must!" When we make demands on other people, on the world around us, on ourselves, we expect that these "wishes" of ours will be taken into account and put into practice. Of course, most often neither other people, nor the world around us, nor even we ourselves are in a hurry to carry out these "orders". As a result, we get angry and complain.

Actually, this is why the requirements traditionally lie at the basis of our irritation.

But "explanations" - in the literal sense of the word - are the strong point of depression. What is the essence of "explanations"? "Explanation" is either an accusation or an excuse. Others, as a rule, are accused by us, and of all serious ones, and our laziness and our fears, of course, are justified by us.

We are running from our problems, but in reality - from life, every day depression takes more and more life from us. We must determine exactly where we are running our flight and stop running. My God, we are running from our own shadow, and this is pure absurdity! This shadow is our life! Where can you run away from her? How can you even run away from it? There is no getting away from it, and to our great, gigantic happiness.

Remember the main thing: the escape is always carried out in the head! And whether you hit the run or not, depends only on you. After all, in the final analysis, "explanation" is only a mental mechanism, nothing more! It can be used by us in any way - both to the detriment and to the benefit of ourselves.

Try to understand this: how you called this or that event, how you explained it, will depend on how you will act.

To identify our depressive "explanations" that involve flight, and to form explanations in ourselves that, on the contrary, will motivate us to be active and productive, is the key to success.

Step 5: Deceive the deceiver

Depression is a great deceiver. She tries to convince us that we do not want anything and, moreover, that we do not even agree with the word "must". Lack of desire is, as we remember, a classic symptom of depression. And depression has a unique weapon against the "must": it says that everything is meaningless, and therefore even the "must" loses all its hypnotic power here.

What to do?! There is only one answer: you need to deceive the deceiver. The psychological technique that we are going to discuss now may seem strange to someone, but this strangeness is due to the only circumstance: one cannot simply agree with depression, it must be deceived.

Imagine an action (deed) that you do not because you consider it important, not because it needs to be done, but "just like that". What can our depression say about this? She will say that it is meaningless, but we do not insist that this action (deed) has any meaning. She will say that she is against any "needs", but we don't need it, we do it - this action (deed) - we do it "just like that".

Above, we discussed the schedule of cases and accomplishments for the day. In it, as we remember, it is easy to detect gaps. What to do with them? The answer, oddly enough, is simple and angry at the same time: we will occupy them with "exploits"! In such an "empty cage" we will plan for ourselves some kind of meaningless act, devoid of purpose and meaning; something we've never done before, or at least haven't done in a long time.

For example, we can make some stew and feed street cats with it. Of course, we will not do this because the cats are starving, and not because we are on probation before enrolling in the Green Party, but simply because we feel like it.

Another example: for no reason, without any serious and meaningful intent, we go to a flower shop and buy some kind of ficus. Then we bring it home, water it, loosen the soil and look for a place to localize our new green friend. I remind you that this action should not be an outrageous act that falls out of the repertoire of our traditional daytime activities and arrangements.

Any such act, carried out by us unplanned, just like that, having nothing to do, for nothing, will produce the effect of an exploding bomb on our psyche. Of course, she - our psyche - will be so excited by this that the release of excess energy sitting in us is simply guaranteed!

And I emphasize once again: by such actions, by our exploits, we simply disarm our own depression. Starting to act just like that, we deprive depression of its noble pathos! She tells us: "Everything is meaningless!" - and we answer: "Thank God, and very good! It is precisely because it is meaningless that we do it! If it made sense, we wouldn't do anything! And so - please! Get it, sign it!"

Lightness, ease, paradoxicality of such a "feat" - this is exactly what we need! Depression itself is absurd, it tries to convince us that we are nothing of ourselves and nothing in this life deserves an opinion at all. Of course, this is complete nonsense!

Step 6: Best reinforcement

First, let's figure out why we do everything we do. Everything we do, we do in order to receive positive reinforcement.

What is positive reinforcement? This is what we enjoy. In order for this or that reflex to become fixed, for this or that habit to form in us, in order for us to do at least something at all, we need positive reinforcement.

Positive reinforcement can range from purely physiological to highly spiritual. Delicious food, sexual pleasure are, of course, positive reinforcements.

In addition, after all, we are not only biological beings, but also social ones, and therefore an unusually significant reinforcement for us is the support and understanding from others, their kind attitude towards us, and in general their presence in our lives.

When we say that we are social beings, we are not talking about the fact that we live in a society, but that we need this society, and we need it biologically.

We feel the need for other people to tell us how good we are. But how rare is such joy!

In the absence of positive reinforcement, depression simply cannot not develop. Positive biological reinforcements in a state of depression disappear simply because we, being in the appropriate - depressive - condition, lose the ability to receive pleasure, and therefore neither food nor sex inspires us and, accordingly, does not reinforce us.

Maybe then we can hope for positive reinforcements from the area of our social life? Let's think, what are the chances of receiving positive reinforcement for a person whose face depicts the mask of grief that is common for a depressed patient? Yes, no chance!

As a result, a person suffering from depression finds himself in a kind of social isolation. But he, more than anyone else, needs the opposite: positive reinforcements are simply vital for him, but in his condition one cannot count on them.

What to do?! It's kind of a vicious circle! But despite all this, there is a solution to this problem.

In fact, although it does not lie on the surface, we are constantly positively reinforcing ourselves, otherwise we would not live at all. In any of our actions, in each act, a positive reinforcement is subconsciously soldered, sewn in.

Here, in fact, this is what has received the name in scientific psychology – "self-reinforcement". And it is this self-reinforcement, as it turns out, that is the only thing without which one cannot get out of the vicious circle.

But in fact it is so easy! And most importantly, there is nothing unnatural and strange in this. We should just start supporting and approving our own actions. In my opinion, this is both logical and correct.

In essence, the technique of this psychotherapeutic technique is quite simple: we just need to reinforce everything we do with positive evaluations. The alarm clock rang, we don't want to get up at all, and we are already sitting on our bed! Well done! We sit well! Then we get up and go to the bathroom, although we don't want to and, as it seems, we can't even, but we're going! Super! Fabulous! Now we brush our teeth, prepare breakfast for ourselves, get ready for work... A feat! Truly a feat! And it turns out, after all, how! A feast for the eyes! Well, you have to get to work somehow, and this is not a pound of raisins for you - public transport, heat or cold, walking march - a throw ... Well done! We manage everything, we can do everything! And at work, as we are at work, we sit well, stand, walk, shift papers from place to place! After all, you still need to be able to do this, you still need to manage it! Very good! We are doing very well! We are great!

Praise yourself, do what others do not do for you, support yourself with a kind word and a good attitude. Realize that you are doing well. Yes, it would probably be possible to move mountains and turn rivers back, but in our case, the smallest deed and the most insignificant accomplishment is a big victory, a victory over depression, a victory over our most sworn enemy! And this, indeed, is worth being judged to the highest standard.

Well, this is probably the simplest and perhaps the most important rule, the most powerful tool in the fight against depression. The ability to create positive reinforcement, self-reinforcement is something that we all must learn without fail, since it is impossible to imagine a better prevention of depression, and one cannot wish for other means of dealing with depression!

Step 7: The blessed word "Enough!"

The fact that you were wasteful, you understand only at the moment of financial collapse. The fact that you were once happy, you realize, only experiencing severe emotional upheavals. Our happiness is always somewhere ahead, in the future or somewhere behind, in the past. And in the daytime with fire it cannot be found in the present! Why? Why don't we know how to be happy even when everything is going well in our life?

Apparently, the whole trouble is in our natural insatiability, we are always short, never enough. We are fed up in one thing, but at the same time we begin to experience hunger in some other part of our living space. Everything is fine at work, which means that at home we are looking for problems. Everything is fine at home - it means that health is a complete bad luck. Everything is in order with health - it means that we do not see the meaning in life. There is no happiness in life!

We urgently need to change tactics! To continue in the same spirit means to doom yourself to constant anxiety and, as a result, to chronic depression. Our psyche is arranged in a sense very primitively, it is busy with the problem of survival, constantly aimed at searching for a potential threat and trying to protect itself from it. As a result, it turns out that by our very nature we are, as it were, aimed at the negative, it is he who is relevant to us.

Let's think about what we're good at. Do you have arms or legs? Fine! Eyes see, ears hear, heart beats? Amazing! Do you have a family, do you have friends, do you have a job (any)? Wonderful! However, this is us by and large, and if we add trifles to this ... So you read a newspaper - this is an opportunity to get information. Say bad? Not true, okay. Here you are sitting now, lying or standing - is that bad too? By no means! Do you still have things to do today? Fine. Nothing to do, can you rest? Better!

In other words, if you take an inventory of everything in your life, it turns out that you are simply the happiest person! Don't you notice it? That's the trouble. Don't you think it's significant? Well, when this "insignificant" is taken away, then you will know that the ability to walk, see, hear, etc. is the most essential that a person can have at all. Want to check it out? Blindfold your eyes, sit like that for an hour - another, and then imagine that this is forever ...

Step 8: Let's change the attitude

"And who is easy now?!" is a phrase deeply rooted in our minds. This is partly true. Problems - heaps! However, it is one thing - difficult life situations that can and should be resolved, another thing - a difficult life situation that has become a psychological problem. Not only did some kind of misfortune happen - family, professional, health let us down - also the soul either went to the heels, or was generally sent on an indefinite vacation in an unknown direction.

Usually, if something happens, we have three ways of reaction ready: anxiety, irritation, or longing. But, as you know, you can't help grief with tears, it's easy to guess from fear, it's also of no use, but there's no need to talk about irritation, just add heat, instead of cooling off for righteous deeds.

Mental health, the ability to use one's psychological potential for one's own needs is not some kind of fun, but an economic factor.

If something has happened, it has already happened; you have to think about what to do with it, how to do the right thing, how to reduce the costs of the trouble that has occurred. If we were fired from work, it is absolutely pointless to grieve, worry about your future or get annoyed with stupid bosses. It is what it is. It's already late, let's go! Now it's business after business: you have to think about where to look for a new job, where to get a job.

Reacting negatively, experiencing, we show miracles of irresponsibility to ourselves! We actually burn through our own opportunities and do not take measures to save our own situation. And if so, then the number of problems increases, and exponentially: you were fired, but you not only lost your salary, you also lost your mental health. And this is our retribution for the fact that we allow ourselves to react negatively to the events that have occurred. Therefore, it turns out that our irresponsibility will call us to responsibility, and wow! We won't be able to pay! Life is ours, there is no one to blame ...

Here, in fact, are all the rules that need to be remembered and implemented when we are faced with life's difficulties. First, do not make problems out of essentially neutral events. Secondly, to perceive an event, which is usually perceived by us in a negative way, as a guide to action: something has happened, which means we need to mobilize and work. Thirdly, you need to remember about your own responsibility for your own life: of course, you can worry and cry, but things will not move from this, and therefore we will have to pay for this.

Chapter 4

P.S. Don't lie to yourself

Now it remains to sort out two feelings that are quite capable of spoiling our lives and which are necessarily included in the picture of our depression. Without them, and this is guilt and aggression, we will not have a depressive state.

When we feel guilty, we think that it is quite justified, because we are at fault. And after all, it doesn't even occur to us: it doesn't get any easier for anyone because of our guilt, on the contrary, it will only get worse.

With aggression, things are even worse. Since it is "not good" to feel anger, and it is impossible not to feel it, we hide our own irritation and by this we injure ourselves, and in the most vile way. Hiding your aggression is a simple matter, but the consequences of this case are catastrophic

So what is guilt? There are two important points here.

Firstly, guilt is a rather strange and unjustified attempt to return to the past and change this past. When a woman says that she is a bad mother, she thinks that she should have raised her child differently, that is, if you remove everything superfluous from here, she dreams of returning to her past and "re-educating" her child, providing him with different conditions life, education, etc. Of course, such a wish, although it seems good, is actually meaningless and serves only one purpose - to bring oneself to a state of severe and impassable depression.

And if we want to get rid of the feeling of guilt, then we must consider the possibility of our return to the past from all sides. Of course, we will come to the conclusion that there is no such possibility. But even after realizing this fact, we still, apparently, will not get rid of guilt. So there is another fact to take into account. Try to answer yourself the question, could the past be different? If you answer yes to this question, then you understand life too simply.

Each event in our life is not your spontaneous decision and not an accident, it is an action dictated by a huge number of a wide variety of external forces and factors beyond our control.

Also, don't confuse your current self with your old self! It's weird to say the least! What you can understand now, from the height of your current experience, your current knowledge and ideas, you could not, and should not have understood then, before, because in the past you had a different experience, other knowledge, other ideas.

In fact, here we traditionally make the same mistake: for some reason we think that then, in the past, we could know how things would end (i.e. what would happen in the future). But, really, if we could know this, then why did we act as if we did not know? I will answer: because we did not know! No one knows what this or that step will lead to, but we take our steps, focusing on what we can focus on.

Secondly, guilt is the other side of megalomania. No - no, don't be scared, this is not about any madness, but simply about our biased attitude towards ourselves. We treat ourselves with prejudice - it's a fact! Do we want to be the best? Yes, definitely (or does anyone want to be the worst?). And how do we like our own mistakes? No, we don't like them, we want to act infallibly. And finally, do we want to make other people happy? Of course, this desire is present in us, we hope that other people will be delighted to communicate with us. So we have all the symptoms of megalomania!

Perhaps, however, I'm exaggerating? But let's listen to our own thoughts in a moment of depression. What are we thinking about? We think that we are nothing of ourselves, i.e., we really want to represent ourselves as something very essential.

Allow yourself to be "nobody". What's so terrible about that? Stop asking yourself to be "the best". Why is this even needed? And if you do this, then be sure: your happiness is guaranteed, especially since, by accepting this terrible alternative that your depression scares you, you will feel strong and free. You will be freed from the illusion of an "ideal" for a normal and fulfilling life.

The second problem here is the feeling of guilt for the mistakes made. But my God, who among us has not made mistakes in his life, who has not done stupid things, who has not acted in a way that should not have been done?! We've all made mistakes, we've all done stupid things, we all have something to blame.

And more than that: we are known to pay for our mistakes, so in general we have every right to them. Giving yourself the right to make a mistake is the most important condition for getting out of depression, and the condition, you see, is completely fair!

And finally, the last thing: the desire to make others happy ... What do we think about in our depression? We think that our loved ones are unhappy through our fault, that we have literally doomed them to the most varied sufferings and torments. But isn't that stupidity?

First, who said they were really unhappy? As a rule, this is a monstrous and unjustified exaggeration, and the most unfortunate in all this "corps de ballet" is the one who blames himself.

Secondly, how is it possible to make anyone happy at all if he himself does not want it, and if he wants to, then in general what can prevent him ?!

Thirdly, it is rather strange to think that people around you must be happy! Leave them the right to choose, stop forcing them!

Let's start with ourselves, let's try to make ourselves happy first, and then we'll think about whether we should take on the rest. However, if we ourselves are happy, believe me, this will be great happiness for those to whom we are dear.

Chapter 5

Epilogue

Yes, depression is a great liar! She paints us an unattainable, impossible, and most importantly, absolutely ridiculous ideal. Of course, we cannot correspond to it (and thank God!), therefore we experience a feeling of deep disappointment in ourselves, we begin to blame ourselves, and then for some reason we are surprised at our bad mood!

In summary, if you really want to manage your depression, you simply must bring common sense, sound reasoning, and most importantly, the ability to separate reality and empty fantasy to your side! And the feeling of guilt is a chimera, it is a game of hide and seek with oneself, it is ultimately the reverse side of our delusions of exclusivity, more precisely, megalomania. It's time to put an end to this, it's time to allow yourself to be a free and contented person, we have every right to do so!